AMY-JILL

ENTERING THE PASSION *of* JESUS

A BEGINNER'S GUIDE to HOLY WEEK

Leader Guide

Alex Joyner

Abingdon Press
Nashville

Entering the Passion of Jesus
A Beginner's Guide to Holy Week
Leader Guide

Copyright © 2018 Abingdon Press
All rights reserved.

978-1-5018-6957-0

18 19 20 21 22 23 24 25 26 27 — 10 9 8 7 6 5 4 3 2 1

MANUFACTURED IN THE UNITED STATES OF AMERICA

CONTENTS

TO THE LEADER

You are beginning a journey. As the leader of this study, you have the opportunity and responsibility to walk with a group of learners on a journey into the story at the heart of the Christian experience—the story of Jesus' Passion. You are not alone! You are going into this journey accompanied by a renowned biblical scholar who will help you and the group come to a deeper understanding of this biblical story. You also have this Leader Guide, which will give you all the ideas you need for six powerful learning sessions.

This Leader Guide is designed to be used with Amy-Jill Levine's book *Entering the Passion: A Beginner's Guide to Holy Week.* Dr. Levine is University Professor of New Testament and Jewish Studies and Mary Jane Werthan Professor of Jewish Studies at Vanderbilt Divinity School and College of Arts and Sciences in Nashville, Tennessee. Besides being an accomplished author and scholar, Dr. Levine is a sought-after speaker who has given hundreds of talks both in the United States and internationally. She brings her Jewish background and her historical expertise in first-century Judaism and Christian origins to her work with the New Testament, and she opens insights into the connections between the Old Testament as well as postbiblical Jewish literature and the Gospels. She is also committed to helping open the Gospels as good news for all people, with a particular interest in what the Gospels say about women.

In this book, Dr. Levine brings her expertise, her story-telling skill and her own love of the Gospels to the last week of Jesus' life. Looking at six different episodes in that dramatic period that Christians call Holy Week, she unearths deep connections between the Jewish tradition that formed Jesus and the events of the Passion. She also helps sets the stage, drawing out the political and religious tensions of Jerusalem in the early 30s of the first century. Dr. Levine also points out the distinctive emphases of each of the four Gospels as they tell the story. She regards the distinct versions of the various events not as contradictions to cast doubt on the story, but as variations on a theme, for the life of Jesus cannot and should not be reduced to a singular perspective.

This Leader Guide provides you with the resources you need to lead this group. It's likely that you have more than enough material. So, you can choose from the options in the "Learning Together" sections to fit the time you have for your group meetings.

There are six sessions in this study, and it makes use of the following components:

- Amy-Jill Levine's book *Entering the Passion of Jesus: A Beginner's Guide to Holy Week,*
- the DVD that accompanies the study, and
- this Leader Guide.

Participants in the study should plan on bringing Bibles and the *Entering the Passion of Jesus* book to each session. If possible, notify those interested in the study in advance of the first session. Make arrangements for them to get copies of the book so they can read the introduction and chapter 1 before the first group meeting.

Using This Guide with Your Group

What will you find in this guide? A session format is below. It is designed to give you options and flexibility in planning your sessions with your group. You will want to develop your sessions with your group in mind. Choose any or all of the activities. Adapt. Reorder. Rearrange. Innovate. Here is the raw material for your lesson planning.

The session plans in this Leader Guide are designed to be completed in a session of about 60–90 minutes in length, but you can use fewer activities to reduce the time to as little as 45 minutes. Depending on which activities you select, there may be special preparation needed. The leader is alerted in the session plan when advance preparation is needed.

Session Format

Planning the Session

Session Goals
Scriptural Foundation
Special Preparation

Getting Started

Opening Activity
Opening Prayer

Learning Together

Video Study and Discussion
Book and Bible Study and Discussion

Wrapping Up

Closing Activity
Closing Prayer

Optional Elements

Journaling

Journaling is a wonderful way to encourage more individual reflection and more extensive interaction outside the group sessions. You can promote the use of a journal by using one of your own as part of your preparation and class time. Group members can use any sort of book they would like for journaling, from a composition book to a bound, blank journal to a set of loose-leaf paper. Encourage those who take on this option to use the journal for reflecting on the reading, writing questions for future learning, and considering commitments they might make for their own spiritual growth. Some of the exercises suggested in the session plans can be done in the journal during class.

Connect with Your Church's Lenten Practices

Entering the Passion of Jesus was created with Lenten practices in mind. Invite your group members to take full part in the Lenten activities in your community of faith. Coordinate with your church leaders to develop a list of opportunities during the Lenten season and consider going as a group to Holy Week activities.

Helpful Hints

Preparing for the Session

1. Pray. You are on an important journey. Pray for God's guidance as you discern and lead. Pray, as well, for the members of your group.
2. Before each session, familiarize yourself with the content. Read the book chapter again.
3. Depending on the length of time you have available for group meetings, you may or may not have time to do all the activities. Select the activities in advance that will work for your group time and interests.
4. Choose the session elements you will use during the group session, including the specific discussion questions you plan to cover. Be prepared, however, to adjust the session as group members interact and as questions arise.
5. Prepare the room where the group will meet so that the space will enhance the learning process. Ideally, group members should be seated around a table or in a circle or semi-circle so that all can see one another. Movable chairs are best because the group will sometimes be forming pairs or small groups for discussion. Special seating arrangements for some sessions are also suggested in the planning notes.

6. Bring a supply of Bibles for those who forget to bring their own.
7. For most sessions you will also need a whiteboard and markers, or an easel with large sheets of paper and markers. You will also see suggestions for preparing large sheets of paper before the sessions.

Shaping the Learning Environment

- Begin and end on time.
- Create a climate of openness, encouraging group members to participate as they feel comfortable.
- Not all members of the group may know one another. Even if people do know one another, have them introduce themselves. They might share a joy or concern; they might talk about what specifically interests them about the Passion narrative (the story of Jesus' last week in Jerusalem); or they might share a Lenten memory, such as giving up a favorite food or walking the Stations of the Cross, seeing a painting depicting one of the scenes associated with the story, or seeing a movie (from classics such as *King of Kings* and *The Greatest Story Ever Told* to more recent films such as *Jesus of Montreal* or Mel Gibson's *The Passion of the Christ*).
- Remember that some people will jump right in with answers and comments, while others need time to process what is being discussed.
- If you notice that some group members seem never to be able to enter the conversation, ask them if they have thoughts to share. Give everyone a chance to talk, but keep the conversation moving. Moderate to prevent a few individuals from doing all the talking.
- Communicate the importance of group discussions and group exercises.
- If no one answers at first during discussions, do not be afraid of silence. Count silently to ten, and then say something such as,

"Would anyone like to go first?" If no one responds, venture an answer yourself and ask for comments.

- Model openness as you share with the group. Group members will follow your example. If you limit your sharing to a surface level, others will follow suit.
- You might share some questions you have of your own—that will help avoid the impression that you know everything (even if you do!).
- Encourage multiple answers or responses before moving on. You can assure participants that there may be more than one good answer to a question, just as there is more than one way to tell the story of Lent (after all, there are four Gospels, and each tells the story in its own way).
- To help continue a discussion and give it greater depth, ask, "Why?" or "Why do you believe that?" or "Can you say more about that?"
- Affirm others' responses with comments such as "Great" or "Thanks" or "Good insight," especially if it's the first time someone has spoken during the group session.
- Monitor your own contributions. If you are doing most of the talking, back off so that you do not train the group to listen rather than speak up.
- Remember that you do not have all the answers. Your job is to keep the discussion going and encourage participation.

Managing the Session

- Honor the schedule. If a session is running longer than expected, get consensus from the group before continuing beyond the agreed-upon ending time.
- Involve group members in various aspects of the group session, such as saying prayers or reading the Scripture.
- Note that the session guides sometimes call for breaking into smaller groups or pairs. This gives everyone a chance to speak

and participate fully. Mix up the groups; don't let the same people pair up for every activity.

- As always in discussions that may involve personal sharing, confidentiality is essential. Group members should never pass along stories that have been shared in the group. Remind the group members at each session: Confidentiality is crucial to the success of this study.

Session 1

JERUSALEM: RISKING REPUTATION

Planning the Session

Session Goals

As a result of conversations and activities connected with this session, group members should begin to

- explore how our expectations determine what we see,
- understand the Old Testament contexts for Jesus' triumphal entry and the political context in which it took place,
- consider the risk Jesus took in entering Jerusalem and how our desire for a hero can lead us to avoid risk, and
- reflect on what we will do for justice in the light of Christ's work.

Scriptural Foundation

The crowds that went ahead of him and that followed were shouting,

"Hosanna to the Son of David!

> *Blessed is the one who comes in the name of the Lord!*
> *Hosanna in the highest heaven!"*
>
> *Matthew 21:9*

Special Preparation

- Prepare the room with seating arranged in a circle so that everyone will be able to see one another.
- Create a small worship space in the center of the circle with visual reminders of God's presence. For this session that could include a candle, an open Bible, a cross, and a small statue or picture of a donkey.
- If this is a new group or you have new members for this study, have name tags available as well as pens and markers.
- Have available paper, pens, pencils, and other drawing materials.
- Also have available Bibles for those who may not have brought one. Encourage participants to bring a Bible for future sessions. Let them know that they can bring whatever version they have (NRSV, NIV, KJV, and so on); sometimes it is helpful to share different translations.
- Post in a visible spot in the room a large piece of paper titled "Events of Holy Week."
- If you have access to a stool and reading stand, have these available for the Reader's Theater exercise.

Getting Started

Opening Activity

As participants arrive, greet them and invite them into a circle of chairs. Especially if it is a newly formed group, have each person write his or her name on a name tag and put it on. Begin the session with brief introductions.

After introductions, say the following to the group: *In this study, we are going to be entering into the stories of the final week of Jesus' earthly life. Each of the four Gospels tells us about this week and it is perhaps the most important story Christians have to tell about who God is. The story of that last week is often called the Passion narrative, with "passion" coming from an old Latin word meaning "to suffer" and "to endure." Jesus' suffering and death reveal to us how God's love works in the world. The Passion narrative is not only about Jesus; it is about his followers as well, and so it is also about us.*

Ask the group members to share, without looking in the study book or a Bible, the events of Jesus' last week as they can remember them. As participants share, write their responses on the large piece of paper titled "Events of Holy Week" that you posted in a visible spot in the room before the session began.

After allowing some time for this exercise, say: *Today we will be focusing on Jesus' entry into Jerusalem, which begins the Passion story. We want to begin by praying that we will see something new that helps us to see the story in a new way, and to see our world differently in light of the story.*

Opening Prayer

Pray together, using the following prayer or one of your own choosing:

God who enters into the suffering of this world, we trust that you see and know the pains of the world and our lives. We share your desire for a world that better reflects your reign, and we ask for new eyes to see your intentions. As we follow Jesus into Jerusalem, upset our expectations and surprise us with new hope for justice and new life. Amen.

Learning Together

Video Study and Discussion

Say to the group: *We will continue our time together with a video featuring Amy-Jill Levine, whom we are going to call "A.-J.," because that's what she prefers. A.-J. will talk about the primary themes of our session today: Jesus' triumphal entry into Jerusalem and the risks taken by Jesus and* his followers. *Notice how A.-J. captures the drama and tension of the scene in her presentation. Make connections to what we have read together in her book. Then, we will discuss both the video and book together.*

Play the first track on the DVD, *Entering the Passion of Jesus*, Session 1: Jerusalem: Risking Reputation (running time is approximately 8–10 minutes).

Say to the group: *Let's keep in mind what A.-J. has said as we take a look at the book and examine these themes in light of our Lenten study.*

Book and Bible Study and Discussion

Discuss the Role of Expectations and the Importance of Details

Invite group members to recall a parade. It could be a famous parade like the ones broadcast on television on Thanksgiving Day or a community parade that happens in your town. Ask the group to finish the following incomplete sentence based on their memories of this parade: "It wouldn't be a parade if it didn't have…" (Some possible answers include marching bands, floats, clowns, and so on.) Allow some time for persons to share responses.

Now say to the group: *A.-J. compares Jesus' entry into Jerusalem to a parade. However, the particular parade the people of Jesus' day had in mind was probably a triumphal entry, which the book describes as a victory parade. The technical term for such a parade is the Greek term* parousia. *You may have heard this term in relation to the return of Jesus at the time of the final judgment.*

Invite the group to read the section of chapter 1 that describes the parades with which the people in Jerusalem, and among those first-century readers of the Gospels, would have been familiar. These include both contemporary parades of generals and kings, and ancient processions such as Solomon's coronation parade. Ask:

- *What elements did these parades have that Jesus' entry also has? What is different?*
- *How did the expectations of the people determine what they saw?*

15

Conduct a Split View Reader's Theater

Make sure that all the participants have access to a Bible for this exercise. Say to the group: *A.-J. emphasizes that we can't fully understand Jesus' entry into Jerusalem unless we know the context from the Old Testament. We're going to conduct a little reader's theater that will help us see the story of Jesus' entry as the Gospel of Matthew describes it alongside stories from the Old Testament that relate to it.*

Divide into four small groups. (If your group is small, this may mean working in pairs. To avoid having one person in a group, you can assign two of the following passages to a group.) Give each group one of the following passages or sets of passages:

1. Zechariah 9:9-10
2. 1 Kings 1:33-40; 2 Kings 9:12-13
3. Psalm 118:19-29
4. Deuteronomy 18:18

Ask each group to read its assigned passage(s) and then read Matthew 21:1-11 to see how the assigned passage sheds light on some element of Matthew's version of Jesus' entry. Encourage the group to use the study book to find additional information about how their assigned verses relate to Matthew's passage. Tell them to prepare to comment on the story as it is read by a narrator.

After the groups have had time to work, ask an individual with a good reading voice to serve as the narrator for a reading of Matthew 21:1-11. Arrange the space so that the narrator is set apart. If you have a stool and reading stand available, place the narrator there.

Ask the small groups to imagine that they are broadcast commentators providing analysis of the story to listeners or viewers. When the narrator pauses, the group members can offer additional information to help interpret what's going on and who the people—the disciples, the crowds— think Jesus is. For instance, after the disciples bring Jesus the donkey and colt, the first group might begin by saying, "Wow! This reminds me of a prophecy in Zechariah. There it says..."

Have the narrator read Matthew's story in the following blocks, pausing after each one for the appropriate group to comment:

1. Matthew 21:1-7
2. Matthew 21:8
3. Matthew 21:9
4. Matthew 21:10-11

Following the reading, thank the participants. Then ask:

- *What surprised you about reading the passage this way?*
- *What do the Old Testament passages tell us about the expectations of who Jesus is?*

Envision Joining the Parade ✓

Read aloud Matthew 21:9-11:

> *The crowds that went ahead of him and that followed were shouting,*
>
> > *"Hosanna to the Son of David!*
> > *Blessed is the one who comes in the name of the Lord!*
> > *Hosanna in the highest heaven!"*
>
> *When he entered Jerusalem, the whole city was in turmoil, asking, "Who is this?" The crowds were saying, "This is the prophet Jesus from Nazareth in Galilee."*

Ask participants:

- *What two titles are given to Jesus in these verses?* [Son of David, prophet]
- *What do they know about his background?* [from Nazareth, in Galilee]

Say to the group: *Both of these titles suggest how the people saw Jesus. According to A.-J., "Son of David" recalls a time when David ruled a nation marked by security and justice, compassion and hope. In calling Jesus a prophet, the crowds were remembering figures like Moses who spoke for God.*

A.-J. wonders what it would mean for us not only to welcome Jesus but al[so] to join the parade and work for the will of God in the world.

We can also reflect on what "Nazareth" and "Galilee" suggest:

- the Christmas story (to remind us that the death of Jesus cannot b[e] separated from his birth and the rest of his life)
- Galilee, and so not a resident of Jerusalem, which is in Judea. Galilee, the place where the mission began and the major miracle[s] occurred.

Divide into small groups of three or four people. Ask the groups [to] read through the section of chapter 1 related to taking up the cross. As[k] them to consider the following questions:

- What did "taking up the cross" mean for the people of Jesus' time? What does it mean for us?
- Why is it important not to separate the Triumphal Entry from the cross?
- Why is it important not to separate the Passion narrative from the rest of the life of Jesus?
- What areas of pain in the world call for risk in the name of justice[?]

After allowing time for discussion, bring the whole group bac[k] together. Share some of the reflections from the small group discussio[n.] Then ask the group members to close their eyes and imagine that they a[re] part of a parade that leads them into the pain of the world and the place[s] where justice and compassion are hard to find. Ask them to respon[d] silently to the following questions, pausing after each one:

- Where are we headed?
- To what or whom are we moving toward?
- Who is moving with us?
- What forces are threatening our progress?
- What might we be called to risk in order to give witness to Christ'[s] cause?
- What gives us courage to keep moving?

Invite group members to draw their vision of the parade using the drawing materials you have provided. Allow time following the exercise for volunteers to share their drawings and visions.

Wrapping Up

Closing Activity

Invite group members to consider the meaning of the word *Hosanna!*, which might be translated as "Save, please!" Read aloud the section of chapter 1 that discusses "Hosanna!" Ask the following question for group discussion:

- *From what did the people who welcomed Jesus need to be saved?*

Now invite group members to reflect silently on a word that describes a situation they would ask Jesus to enter for salvation. Ask them to write that word on a piece of paper.

Closing Prayer

If the group is using a common biblical translation, invite them to read aloud Psalm 118. Alternatively, ask a good reader to read it aloud. Remind the group of the author's reminder that the psalm describes a promise of God that is available every day.

As an act of prayer, invite volunteers to say aloud the word they have written down in the previous exercise followed by the group saying the word *Hosanna!* One model of the prayer is:

Lord, who risks the difficult path of sacrifice,
we welcome you with our cries to save, as the people met you in
Jerusalem.
Hear our cries of "Hosanna!"

[Individuals offer their word, followed by the group saying "Hosanna!" After all have had an opportunity to share, continue . . .]

Blessed is the One who comes in the name of the Lord. Hosanna in the highest. Amen!

Session 2

THE TEMPLE: RISKING RIGHTEOUS ANGER

Planning the Session

Session Goals

As a result of conversations and activities connected with this session, group members should begin to

- understand the different emphases that the Gospels attach to the Temple incident;
- appreciate the role of the Temple in Jewish and Christian thought;
- consider how Jesus' actions in the Temple can be used to challenge notions of hospitality, grace, the role of money in contemporary churches, and the problems that happen when churches are places where sinners feel relaxed rather than repentant; and
- develop strategies for turning feelings of anger at injustice into action.

Scriptural Foundation

Then they came to Jerusalem. And he entered the temple and began to drive out those who were selling and those who were

*buying in the temple, and he overturned the tables of the
money changers and the seats of those who sold doves; and he
would not allow anyone to carry anything through the temple.
He was teaching and saying, "Is it not written,*

> *'My house shall be called a house of prayer for all the
> nations'?
> But you have made it a den of robbers."*
>
> Mark 11:15-17

Special Preparation

- Prepare the room with seating arranged in a circle so that everyone will be able to see one another.
- Create a small worship space in the center of the circle with
  visual reminders of God's presence. For this session, that could
  include a whip and some scattered coins (preferably coins from
  other nations, such as euros, sen, yen, and pesewas).
- Have available paper, pens, pencils, and other drawing
  materials.
- Also have available Bibles for those who may not have brought
  one.
- Prepare two pieces of paper or card stock. On one write the
  words: *A House of Prayer for All Nations.* On the other write:
  A Den of Robbers. Post the signs in a visible place in your
  meeting area.
- If you have access to Bible dictionaries, have them available for
  participants to use.
- Prepare a chart on a large, blank sheet of paper. The chart
  should have three columns and five rows. The heading for the
  second column should say "Mark" and the heading for the third
  column should say "John." In the first column, beginning with
  the second row write the following, each in its own cell:
  o *Where in Gospel*
  o *What Jesus does*
  o *What Jesus says*
  o *Result*

- Post a large, blank sheet of paper in a visible, accessible spot in your meeting space.

Getting Started

Opening Activity

Remember

Read aloud Isaiah 56:6-8:

> And the foreigners who join themselves to the LORD,
> > to minister to him, to love the name of the LORD,
> > and to be his servants,
> all who keep the sabbath, and do not profane it,
> > and hold fast my covenant—
> these I will bring to my holy mountain,
> > and make them joyful in my house of prayer;
> their burnt offerings and their sacrifices
> > will be accepted on my altar;
> for my house shall be called a house of prayer
> > for all peoples.
> Thus says the LORD God,
> > who gathers the outcasts of Israel,
> I will gather others to them
> > besides those already gathered.

✓ Then direct the group's attention to the sign you posted earlier that says "A House of Prayer for All Nations." Ask:

- *What does this way of describing the Temple imply for how we should act toward people who are not members of our church? to people who are not Christians? to people who are of different ethnicities?*

- *What parts of our church life help us live into being "A House of Prayer for All Nations"?*

Now invite the group to reflect silently on these additional questions:

- *With whom do we, as individuals and as this church, need to be reconciled?*
- *How is God's embrace of those have a different way of worshiping than we do good news for us?*

Opening Prayer

Read the following prayer, or one of your own, aloud:

God of the Passover,
who brought to freedom those who passed through the waters of the
Red Sea,
and raised again to life Jesus from the dead,
We look for your reconciling love that makes us one,
and we long for the courage to risk living out of that love.
Bless us now as we gather around your Living Word. Amen.

Learning Together

Video Study and Discussion

Say to the group: *We will continue our time together with a video featuring A.-J. Levine. A.-J. will talk about the primary themes of our session today: Jesus' disruption in the Temple (also known as the "cleansing of the Temple") and the risks taken by Jesus as he expresses his anger. Notice how A.-J. describes the Temple setting in detail. Make connections to what we have read together in her book. Then, we will discuss both the video and book together.*

Play the second track on the DVD, *Entering the Passion of Jesus*, Session 2: The Temple: Risking Righteous Anger (running time is approximately 8–10 minutes).

Say to the group: *Let's keep in mind what A.-J. has said as we take a look at the book and examine these themes in light of our Lenten study.*

Book and Bible Study and Discussion

Explore the Meaning of the Temple

Say to the group: *The Temple was an important site for the Jewi*
people in Jesus' time, including the followers of Jesus such as Peter and Pau
Let's explore what it meant and continued to mean.

Divide into four small groups. Give each group one of the followir
questions to explore, using chapter 2 in the study guide as a resourc
If you have other resources available, like a Bible dictionary, encouras
participants to use those as well.

1. *Who was welcome at the Temple?*
2. *Why were there vendors at the Temple?*
3. *How did Jesus' followers feel about the Temple?*
4. *What was the environment like in the Temple during the Passove*
   (for example, noisy v. quiet)

After allowing some time for small group work, bring the whole grou
back together. Invite each group to share their learnings. Ask the group

- *What further questions do you have about Temple worship?*

Invite volunteers to do further exploration on these questions an
report back to a future session of the group.

Investigate the Repercussions of the Temple Incident

Divide once again into two smaller groups. Assign each group one o
the following passages:

1. Mark 11:15-19
2. John 2:13-22

Using their assigned passage and chapter 2 in the study book, as
each group to answer the following questions:

- *Where does this passage appear in the Gospel [that is, near the*
  beginning, middle, or end]?

- *What does Jesus do in this passage?*
- *What does Jesus say?*
- *What is the result of this incident?*

Reconvene the whole group after allowing some time for them to work. Say to the group: *Three of the Gospels (Matthew, Mark, and Luke), tell a very similar story of the Temple incident, sometimes called the cleansing of the Temple. We call these three Gospels the Synoptics, which comes from a Greek word meaning "to see together." John has some distinct differences. Let's look at this story from one of the Synoptics and compare it with John's version.*

(For reference, the other descriptions in the Synoptics are found in Matthew 21:12-17 and Luke 19:45-48.)

Using the chart you posted before the session began, fill in the grid using information shared by the two groups. After each group has had a chance to share, ask:

- *How do these accounts differ?*
- *What does each contribute to our picture of the Temple?*
- *What does each contribute to our picture of Jesus?*

Consider Caiaphas's Challenge

Read aloud the section of chapter 2 that discusses Caiaphas's challenge. Ask the group the following questions:

- *What were the responsibilities of Caiaphas as the high priest in Jerusalem?*
- *Why could his position be considered "between a rock and a hard place"?*
- *Have we ever had to give up our own privilege or rights for the sake of the group? Have we ever been asked to do so?*
- *How do our responsibilities sometimes prevent us from risking a more courageous option?*

25

Consider Churches and Comfort

Direct the group's attention to the other sign you posted before the session began, which says "A Den of Robbers." Read aloud the section of chapter 2 that talks about this phrase.

Say to the group: *A.-J. notes that a "den of robbers" or a cave of thieves is a place where thieves feel safe. When Jesus called the Temple "a den of robbers," his concern was people coming to the Temple and not being challenged to be transformed by God's grace.*

Invite group members to consider how your faith community both welcomes people and calls them to transformation. Write responses on the large, blank sheet of paper you posted before the session began as you ask:

- *Why does Jesus disrupt the comfort many people experienced in the Temple?*
- *What are the challenges our church faces in welcoming people who are not already "insiders"?*
- *How could we welcome people more fully?*
- *How does our church worship and church life call us to be transformed by God's grace?*

Analyze the Offering in Your Church

If the group members attend the same worship service together, spend some time describing how the collection is done at that service. How is this time described in the order of worship? What words are said? Who comes forward? What happens while the offering is conducted? How is the offering presented? If you have a bulletin from a service, note what is listed for this section of the service. If group members do not attend a common service, have volunteers describe the offering practices in their settings. Ask:

- *What are we communicating about the role of money in our lives and in the church by the way we practice the offering?*
- *What might a non-Christian think about the rituals surrounding the offering (collection plates or baskets, envelopes, the music, the people who take up the collection and bring it forward, and so on)?*

- *How do we make rich and poor feel welcome in our church?*
- *In what ways are we challenged to reflect on how we make and use money in other parts of our lives?*
- *In what ways are we challenged to think about how the church uses the money taken up in the collection?*

Turn Anger into Action

Read aloud the section of chapter 2 in which A.-J. discusses anger. Then invite group members to find a partner for the next exercise. Ask the pairs to choose which person will share first. Then ask those sharing to tell a story about a time when they were angry and reacted in a way that they later regretted. (Assure them that they do not have to share a deep, dark secret or major act!) Tell the people sharing that they will have one minute to share this story while the other person in the pair listens.

After one minute, have the partners switch roles and share on the same topic. Again, time the sharing and let them know when time is up.

Now ask them to share again, this time telling of a time when they were angry and reacted in a way that felt appropriate. Again, allow one minute for each partner to share.

Draw the group back together and ask:

- *When does anger become problematic or sinful?*
- *When is it appropriate to disrupt someone else's comfort because of our anger?*
- *How can we turn our anger into actions that do not hurt but help?*

Distribute pieces of paper and writing instruments to participants. Invite group members to write or draw on the paper a situation in the world that makes them angry by disturbing their moral conscience. Allow time for persons to work and then ask them to respond to the following questions by writing answers on their paper:

- *Who needs to have their comfort disturbed in order to address this situation?*
- *What would I have to risk in order to address this situation?*
- *What is one thing I could do this week to move toward changing this situation?*

Wrapping Up

Closing Activity

Ask group members to close their eyes and get comfortable in their chairs as you lead them through a body exercise. Say to the group *Sometimes we can feel in our body our reactions to injustice. As you keep your eyes closed, imagine a situation in the world that causes you anger. [Pause] Feel in your body where you are holding the stress this situation causes you. [Pause] Now, make fists out of your hands. Feel the strength God has given you to move and act. Squeeze into your fists. [Pause] Now, relax your hands and arms and let them fall to your side. Let go of the stress you feel in your limbs, your neck, your face. Trust that God is with you and will act to bring justice and redemption. [Pause]*

At the close of the exercise, invite persons to open their eyes.

Closing Prayer

Offer the following prayer or one of your own:

Mess-making Jesus,
*   As you did in the temple,*
*   You disturb our comfort by challenging us to change.*
You know how hard it is for trust
*   But you also know how easily we fall into despair*
*   Or spend ourselves in destructive anger.*
We need a savior who will show us the path to life.
So we follow you on this Passion journey
*   To the temple and beyond. Amen.*

Session 3

TEACHINGS:
RISKING CHALLENGE

Planning the Session

Session Goals

As a result of conversations and activities connected with this session, group members should begin to

- identify the tensions on display in the challenges to Jesus' teaching in the Temple,
- consider the implications of Jesus' teachings for our own Lenten reflections,
- understand the Great Commandment as it relates to other sections of Old Testament Law, and
- explore the meaning of taxes in the context of Jesus' day and in our own times.

Scriptural Foundation

One of the scribes came near and heard them disputing with one another, and seeing that he answered them well, he asked him, "Which commandment is the first of all?" Jesus answered, "The first is, 'Hear, O Israel: the Lord our God, the Lord is one;

you shall love the Lord your God with all your heart, and with all your soul, and with all your mind, and with all your strength.' The second is this, 'You shall love your neighbor as yourself.' There is no other commandment greater than these."

Mark 12:28-31

Special Preparation

- Prepare the room with seating arranged in a circle so that everyone will be able to see one another.
- Create a small worship space in the center of the circle with visual reminders of God's presence. For this session that could include two pennies or other coins of small denomination.
- Have available paper, pens, pencils, and other drawing materials.
- Also have available Bibles for those who may not have brought one.
- For the opening activity, "Consider the Meaning of Money," have available a few one dollar bills for group members to use (and return!) for the exercise if they do not have one of their own.
- On a large piece of paper, print the phrase *"You don't die by the Law but live by the Law."* Post the phrase in a prominent place in your meeting area.
- On a large piece of paper, create a chart with two columns. Label one column "Pharisees" and the other column "Herodians." Post the chart in a visible, accessible place in your meeting area.

Getting Started

Opening Activity

Consider the Meaning of Money

Ask participants to pull out a dollar (or other bill or coin) to look at. If some persons do not have money with them, share dollar bills that you brought with you for the session or have them look on with someone else who does have money.

Say to the group: *In this session, we will be reviewing two times when money was a part of Jesus' teaching in the Temple. Money plays a significant role in our lives, even if we feel we have too little of it. Let's spend [!] a minute looking at the piece of money in front of us. And we can even stop here to recall that terms regarding money impact our language: we spent time, and we spend money. What we "spend" is usually something of value.*

Invite group members to observe the currency in front of them. Ask them to note their answers to the following questions in silence:

- *What are the most prominent images on this currency?*
- *What words are most prominent?*
- *How do the words and images make me feel about the country that issued this currency?*

Now invite group reflection on the following questions:

- *What do the words and images on this currency say about what we value as a country?*
- *What does this currency say about who we are and what we stand for?*
- *How much of a claim do these values have on us as people who carry and use this money?*

Opening Prayer

Read the following prayer aloud, or use one of your own:

We are following you, Jesus, down paths that challenge our allegiances and risk our comforts.
We are watching to see what you will do.
Will you say the expected thing or do the unexpected?
Will you be true to whom we assume you are
  Or will you surprise us once again?
We see the costly journey of your Passion
  And we wonder at the risks you took.

We want to believe like you believe
　　In the power of God's love. Amen.

Learning Together

Video Study and Discussion

Say to the group: *We will continue our time together with a video featuring A.-J. Levine. A.-J. will talk about the primary themes of our session today: Jesus' teachings in the Temple and the risks he takes in delivering his message and confronting challengers. Note how A.-J. also describe additional aspects of his teachings. Make connections to what we have read together in her book. Then, we will discuss both the video and book together*

Play the third track on the DVD, *Entering the Passion of Jesus Session 3: Teachings: Risking Challenge* (running time is approximately 8–10 minutes).

Say to the group: *Let's keep in mind what A.-J. has said as we take a look at the book and examine these themes in light of our Lenten study.*

Book and Bible Study and Discussion

Explore the Old Testament Roots of the Greatest Commandment

Read aloud Mark 12:28-34:

> *One of the scribes came near and heard them disputing with one another, and seeing that he answered them well, he asked him, "Which commandment is the first of all?" Jesus answered, "The first is, 'Hear, O Israel: the Lord our God, the Lord is one; you shall love the Lord your God with all your heart, and with all your soul, and with all your mind, and with all your strength.' The second is this, 'You shall love your neighbor as yourself.' There is no other commandment greater than these." Then the scribe said to him, "You are right, Teacher; you have truly said that 'he is one, and besides him there is no other'; and 'to love him with all the heart, and with all the understanding, and with all the strength,' and 'to love one's*

neighbor as oneself,'—this is much more important than all whole burnt offerings and sacrifices." When Jesus saw that he answered wisely, he said to him, "You are not far from the kingdom of God." After that no one dared to ask him any question.

Say to the group: *Jesus sums up the Law by lifting up two Old Testament commands as primary: loving God and loving our neighbor. Let's look at the places in the Old Testament where we find those commands.*

Distribute Bibles to those who have not brought their own and divide into two groups. Ask one group to turn to Deuteronomy 6 and look for the command to love God. Have the other group turn to Leviticus 19 and look for the command to love one's neighbor. Ask both groups to explore the following questions about their assigned chapter:

- *What verses contain the command you are looking for?*
- *Given the context, why does this command seem important?*
- *What other kinds of love are talked about in this chapter?*

After allowing some time for the small group work, bring the whole group back together and ask:

- *What did you learn about what it means to love God or your neighbor?*
- *If we took these commands seriously, what would have to change in our lives? in our churches?*
- *What would we have to risk if we took these commandments more seriously?*

Discuss the Meaning of the Greatest Commandment

Read aloud the section of chapter 3 in which A.-J. discusses how to understand loving God and loving neighbor as the "greatest" of all the commandments. Direct the group's attention to the phrase you posted on the wall prior to the session that says "You don't die by the Law but live by the Law." Ask:

- *How does A.-J. suggest using the Great Commandment when it seems the Law has conflicting demands?*
- *What does it mean to "die by the Law"?*
- *What does it mean to "live by the Law"?*
- *When has following God's commands helped you feel freedom or joy?*

Reenact the Story of the Poor Widow in the Temple

Read aloud Mark 12:41-44:

> He sat down opposite the treasury, and watched the crowd putting money into the treasury. Many rich people put in large sums. A poor widow came and put in two small copper coins, which are worth a penny. Then he called his disciples and said to them, "Truly I tell you, this poor widow has put in more than all those who are contributing to the treasury. For all of them have contributed out of their abundance; but she out of her poverty has put in everything she had, all she had to live on."

Ask for several volunteers (at least six) to do an improvisational reenactment of the story of the widow's mite. Assign the following roles:

- Jesus, who is teaching in the temple,
- several rich people,
- a widow with two small coins, and
- several disciples sitting with Jesus.

Give the group of volunteers one minute to prepare their improvisation based on the Gospel text you have read. Then ask them to perform their improv for the group.

After they have finished, thank the group for their work and ask:

- *What did you notice in the improv that you may not have noticed in the reading?*
- *What are we supposed to think about the widow?*

- *In what ways is her gift a sign of what Jesus is giving in his Passion journey?*

Now read the section of chapter 3 in which A.-J. discusses the system reciprocity that governed the offering system in the Temple. Ask:

- *Why is this story about more than the widow's self-sacrifice?*
- *How did the Temple system support the poor?*
- *What kind of support does your faith community offer to its most vulnerable members and other vulnerable people in the community?*
- *What more could it do?*

onsider the Pharisees and Herodians

Read aloud Mark 12:13-17:

> *Then they sent to him some Pharisees and some Herodians to trap him in what he said. And they came and said to him, "Teacher, we know that you are sincere, and show deference to no one; for you do not regard people with partiality, but teach the way of God in accordance with truth. Is it lawful to pay taxes to the emperor, or not? Should we pay them, or should we not?" But knowing their hypocrisy, he said to them, "Why are you putting me to the test? Bring me a denarius and let me see it." And they brought one. Then he said to them, "Whose head is this, and whose title?" They answered, "The emperor's." Jesus said to them, "Give to the emperor the things that are the emperor's, and to God the things that are God's." And they were utterly amazed at him.*

Say to the group: *Jesus is aware of the hypocrisy of those who question im, but the Pharisees and Herodians had interests that are familiar to us. .et's look at who they were.*

Now read aloud the section of chapter 3 that discusses the Pharisees nd the Herodians testing Jesus with a question about taxes. Using the

chart you prepared before the session began, invite group members
describe the Pharisees and the Herodians based on the reading. Wri
responses in the appropriate columns on the chart. Ask:

- *What were the interests of each group?*
- *How do you think each would answer the question that they ask Jesus?*
- *In what ways are we asking similar questions today?*

Reflect on Our Use of Money

Distribute pieces of paper and writing instruments to the participan
Invite them to create a log of their spending over the past twenty-fo
hours, noting how much they spent on each item and where they spe
it. (If some participants didn't spend any money in the past twenty-fo
hours, they can expand the period as it makes sense to them.) Assu
them that they will not be asked to share the log with the group.

After giving the group time for this exercise, ask them to reflect c
the following questions:

- *How typical a day was this in terms of your spending habits?*
- *What does this log reveal about what you value?*
- *To whom or what are we giving our money?*

Say to the group: *A.-J. says that the New Testament offers various wa
to answer the question of what it means to "give to the emperor the thin,
that are the emperor's, and to God the things that are God's"* (Mark 12:17
We are challenged to answer the same question.

Invite the group, using the same piece of paper, to do some reflectio
on how they could take one significant step toward giving more to Go
Use the following questions to guide your reflection:

- *What would giving more to God look like?*
- *How would this giving honor God?*
- *What might we, as individuals and as a church, have to risk in th giving?*

- *How would it change our thinking about the significance of money for us?*

After allowing some time for individual work, ask for volunteers to share their thoughts on the exercise, including any steps they might take. Do not force sharing, however. Invite participants to take their intended step home with them and to place it in a location they will see each day, such as next to their bathroom mirror or on the refrigerator. Encourage them to come back for the next session and report on how they've done in following through and what the change [again, a monetary term!] has meant to them.

Wrapping Up

Closing Activity

Meditate on Love

Say to the group: *Jesus' teachings in the Temple challenge us to think about what we love and how we can love God and neighbor more. We sometimes know we have love only when it is tested. And in those times of testing, we can trust the love that Jesus had that offers our raw honesty to God.*

Invite the group members to spend a few minutes in silence reflecting on areas in their own lives where they feel their love is being tested. What would you tell God about the challenges you are facing? Whom do you need to love more?

Closing Prayer

Offer the following prayer or one of your own:

God of love,
Who walked the journey of life and death with us,
In Jesus you were tested and tried.
When we are tested and tried,
Help us remember the love in which we were created,
And which is never ending. Amen.

Session 4

THE FIRST DINNER: RISKING REJECTION

Planning the Session

Session Goals

As a result of conversations and activities connected with this session, group members should begin to

- understand the different roles women play in the story of Jesus and his disciples,
- appreciate the different roles of anointing in the Bible,
- consider the nature of our giving to the poor and what it means to give to what we think is good, and
- reflect on our motives for following Jesus.

Scriptural Foundation

Now while Jesus was at Bethany in the house of Simon the leper, a woman came to him with an alabaster jar of very costly ointment, and she poured it on his head as he sat at the table. But when the disciples saw it, they were angry and said, "Why this waste? For this ointment could have been sold for a large sum, and the money given to the poor." But Jesus, aware of this, said to them, "Why do you trouble the woman? She has performed a good service for me. For you always have the poor with you, but you will not always have me. By pouring this ointment on my body she has prepared me for burial. Truly I tell you, wherever this good news is proclaimed in the whole world, what she has done will be told in remembrance of her."

Matthew 26:6-13

Special Preparation

- Prepare the room with seating arranged in a circle so that everyone will be able to see one another.
- Create a small worship space in the center of the circle with visual reminders of God's presence. For this session, that could include a perfume jar and a bottle of olive oil.
- Have available paper, pens, pencils, and other drawing materials.
- Also have available Bibles for those who may not have brought one.
- Have a small dish and olive oil available for use in the opening activity.
- Have cups or glasses and sparkling grape juice or water for a "Last Supper."
- On a large sheet of paper, write the following heading: *Words Associated with Anointing*. Now write down the left side of the paper the following three words: *christos*, *mashiach*, and *myrizo*. Post the paper in a visible, accessible location in your meeting area.

Getting Started

Opening Activity

Remember the Anointing

Say to the group: *As we continue our Lenten journey together with Jesus, today we are going to recall the woman who anointed Jesus. As we will see,*

the Gospels tell various versions of this story that emphasize different themes.
Listen as we read Matthew's version for how Jesus and the disciples respond
to the woman's act.

Read aloud (or have a good reader read aloud) Matthew 26:6-13:

> *Now while Jesus was at Bethany in the house of Simon the*
> *leper, a woman came to him with an alabaster jar of very*
> *costly ointment, and she poured it on his head as he sat at*
> *the table. But when the disciples saw it, they were angry and*
> *said, "Why this waste? For this ointment could have been sold*
> *for a large sum, and the money given to the poor." But Jesus,*
> *aware of this, said to them, "Why do you trouble the woman?*
> *She has performed a good service for me. For you always*
> *have the poor with you, but you will not always have me. By*
> *pouring this ointment on my body she has prepared me for*
> *burial. Truly I tell you, wherever this good news is proclaimed*
> *in the whole world, what she has done will be told in*
> *remembrance of her."*

Ask:

- *How do the disciples respond to the woman?*
- *How does Jesus respond?*
- *How do we respond to some good act done for us?*

Invite the group into a simple act of anointing. Pour some olive oil
into a small dish. Then tell the group that you are going to invite them
to receive an anointing as a small blessing. Explain that you will anoint
the hand of the person to your left by making the sign of the cross with
your thumb. Then you will say to the person: *May the peace of Christ*
be with you.

After the person has received the anointing and blessing, invite that
person to repeat the act with the person on the left until you have gone
around the circle. If for any reason some people would not like to receive
the anointing, instruct them to place their hands in their laps and simply
receive the words of blessing.

Opening Prayer

Read the following prayer aloud, or use one of your own:

God of Extravagant Giving,
You bless us with the impulse to respond to suffering with care.
Like the woman who anointed Jesus,
You give costly gifts so that we can know blessings.
Help us not to offer you gifts that cost us nothing.
Help us to risk being generous,
And help us to see your image in the face of everyone we meet. Amen.

Learning Together

Video Study and Discussion

Say to the group: *We will continue our time together with a video featuring A.-J. Levine. A.-J. will talk about the primary themes of our session today: the anointing of Jesus and the role of women in his ministry. Pay close attention to how A.-J. describes the women who followed Jesus. Make connections to what we have read together in her book. Then, we will discuss both the video and book together.*

Play the fourth track on the DVD, *Entering the Passion of Jesus, Session 4: The First Dinner: Risking Rejection* (running time is approximately 8–10 minutes).

Say to the group: *Let's keep in mind what A.-J. has said as we take a look at the book and examine these themes in light of our Lenten study.*

Book and Bible Study and Discussion

Hold a First Supper

Say to the group: *Matthew and Mark both tell us that the story of the woman who anoints Jesus will be told in remembrance of her, yet this story, which these two Gospels place within the Passion story, is often not featured during Holy Week. A.-J. says that perhaps we ought to include in our Lenten practice a "First Supper" to remember such unnamed women in Jesus'*

journey. In memory of this story, we're going to recreate the conversation th
might happen at such a supper.

Divide into four groups. Assign each group one of the four Gosp
stories that tell the story of Jesus' anointing:

1. Matthew 26:6-13
2. Mark 14:3-9
3. Luke 7:36-50
4. John 12:1-7

Ask the small groups to pay attention to the details in the story usin
the following questions to guide their discussion:

- *Who is the woman who anoints Jesus and what do we know about her?*
- *Why does she anoint Jesus?*
- *What more do you wonder about her?*
- *How do Jesus and those around him respond to her?*

While the groups are working, prepare cups or glasses of sparklin
grape juice or water for each person present.

After giving the groups time to work, bring the whole group bac
together and give each person a cup or glass. Say to the group member
*Now imagine that we are at dinner where we are some of the origin
disciples of Jesus who are remembering his story, but imagine that the versic
of the anointing that you have studied is the only one you know. Let's tai
with one another about what we remember.*

Use the following questions to guide the conversation:

- *Who was that woman who anointed Jesus?*
- *Why did she do it?*
- *Who first responded to her action, and what did they say?*
- *How did Jesus respond to them?*
- *What do you imagine Jesus said to her?*
- *What do you imagine happened to her?*

Close the conversation by offering a toast to the woman.

Research Different Kinds of Anointing

Direct the group's attention to the words related to anointing on the large sheet of paper titled *"Words Associated with Anointing"* that you prepared before the session began. Ask the group to search chapter 4 of the study book to find the meanings for each of the three terms—*christos, mashiach,* and *myrizo.* As participants volunteer definitions, write them next to the appropriate words on the sheet.

Now ask for volunteers to look at the following verses and identify what kind of anointing is being described:

1. 1 Samuel 10:1
2. 1 Samuel 16:13
3. 1 Kings 1:39
4. 2 Kings 9:6
5. Mark 14:8

Ask:

- *How does Jesus' anointing differ from the other anointings?*
- *How does Jesus' anointing signal that he is a different kind of king?*
- *What might it mean that a woman does the anointing?*
- *What risks did the woman face at this dinner?*
- *What risks did Jesus face at this dinner?*

Debate a Gift of Beauty

Invite the group to imagine that they are members of a memorials committee at a local church. Say to the group: *A member of the church, whom you know is in a financially precarious situation, has received a large amount of money from the estate of a relative. She knows that the church has been planning a big project to refurbish and beautify the stained glass windows and chancel area of the sanctuary. She approaches you, as members of the memorials committee, to give you most of the money needed for that project. She does not ask for any recognition for herself or her family, such as engraved plaques or names in the windows.*

You are tasked with receiving this gift. Half of you are elated that the project can go forward and are ready to receive the gift joyfully. The other half of you are concerned that the woman is making her financial situation worse by not using at least some of the money for her needs.

Divide the group into two smaller groups, each representing one of the two positions outlined. Have them huddle to talk about how they would defend their position. Have them use the following questions to guide their discussion:

- *What biblical stories or teachings support your position?*
- *What would Jesus do?*

Now have the two groups come back together in character and discuss the proposed gift. At the end of a period of discussion, have someone from each group summarize the position presented by the other group.

Then say: *A.-J. says that if the Gospels open up moral questions they are doing their job. How does this situation help us think about the role of giving to something that we see as a good? How does it help us consider our responsibility to those in need?*

Examine Our Motives for Following Jesus

Read aloud the section of chapter 4 in which A.-J. discusses the possible motives the women in the Gospel stories had for following Jesus. Ask:

- *What is something new you learned about the options women had in following Jesus?*
- *How does it change your impression of the role of women to know that some had funds to support Jesus?*
- *Why might they have followed Jesus?*
- *What might they have done along with providing financial gifts?*

Now invite group members to reflect on their own motives for following Jesus. Distribute pieces of paper and writing instruments to each participant. Ask them to turn the paper horizontally (landscape mode) and to create a time line of their lives with birth being at the left side of the page and the current day being at the right. Ask them to reflect on moments in their life when they became aware that they were following Jesus "on purpose." Ask:

- *What sort of expectations, if any, did you grow up with about following Jesus?*
- *What were the key moments in your faith journey?*
- *What did those moments looks like?*
- *How did your life change following these moments?*
- *How did other people—friends, family, co-workers, neighbors—feel about your change? What did you risk?*

After allowing some minutes for individual work, invite volunteers to share their time lines. Do not force sharing. Assure the group that we are all at different places in our faith journeys, but asking ourselves why we are at the stage we're in can be a useful way of considering what our next step might be.

Wrapping Up

Closing Activity

Remember the People Important to You

Invite the group to reflect on the time line they created in the earlier activity. Ask them to consider silently the people who were important in their lives at the times when their faith was growing. Ask:

- *Who challenged you to see something new?*
- *Who helped you name something within yourself that you found hard to name?*
- *Who helped you see a larger purpose for your life?*
- *Did someone you did not know, or did not know well, ever give you a gift you did not expect? How did that make you feel?*

Take the small dish with the olive oil that you used in the opening activity. Hold it in your hands and explain the next part of the exercise: *Let's give thanks for the people we have been thinking about by naming them aloud. As the dish is passed around this time, speak those names and pass it to the next person. We will repeat until everyone has had a chance to share.*

Closing Prayer

Read the following prayer aloud, or use one of your own:

God who blesses us with community,
We give thanks for the people whose names we have spoken.
We give thanks that we do not walk this Lenten journey alone.
And we pray that we may take the risk of blessing as well.
In Jesus' name. Amen.

Session 5

THE LAST SUPPER: RISKING THE LOSS OF FRIENDS

Planning the Session

Session Goals

As a result of conversations and activities connected with this session, group members should begin to

- connect the Gospel narratives of the Last Supper to Old Testament traditions of Passover and the sacrificial system,
- appreciate the complexity of two major characters in the Passion story—Peter and Judas,
- reflect on foot washing as an act of humble service, and
- consider our own responses to injustice and our impulse to give and receive service.

Scriptural Foundation

Then he poured water into a basin and began to wash the disciples' feet and to wipe them with the towel that was tied around him. He came to Simon Peter, who said to him, "Lord, are you going to wash my feet?" Jesus answered, "You do not

> know now what I am doing, but later you will understand."
> Peter said to him, "You will never wash my feet." Jesus
> answered, "Unless I wash you, you have no share with me."
> Simon Peter said to him, "Lord, not my feet only but also my
> hands and my head!"
>
> John 13:5-9

Special Preparation

- Prepare the room with seating arranged in a circle so that everyone will be able to see one another.
- Create a small worship space in the center of the circle with visual reminders of God's presence. For this session, that could include a basin, towel, chalice, rooster, and a bag of coins.
- Have a good, unsliced loaf of bread available and a good, gluten-free bread option for those who may need it. The bread can be sweet (such as cinnamon raisin bread) or savory (such as ciabatta) but it should be moist and easy to tear pieces from.
- Have available a small container of hand sanitizers and some napkins.
- Have available paper, pens, pencils, and other drawing materials.
- Also have available Bibles for those who may not have brought one.
- On an index card, write the following questions:
  o *What was the oppression that concerned God?*
  o *What was God doing to address it?*
  o *What was the purpose of the Passover sacrifice?*
- On another index card, write these questions:
  o *What does John the Baptizer call Jesus in this passage?*
  o *How does this title relate to the Passover story in Exodus 12?*
  o *How does this understanding of who Jesus is change the understanding of the Passover offering?*

Getting Started

Opening Activity

Remember a Special Meal

After everyone has arrived, invite them to find a partner (preferably someone they do not know too well) and to decide which of the two of them would like to go first in this exercise. Say to the group: *I'd like to ask you to remember a special meal in your family. It might have been for a holiday, like Thanksgiving or Christmas, or for a special occasion in your family. Think about who was present, what kind of food was on the table, and any special words that were said. Where did you sit? Who did the preparations?*

Now announce that you will give each person 90 seconds to share, beginning with the partner who elected to go first. The other person should listen as the first partner shares. Track the time and after 90 seconds inform the pairs that it is time to switch roles. Then after another 90 seconds call the whole group back together.

Ask the group to reflect on the following questions:

- *How were the special meals different from your everyday meals?*
- *Why do you think meals are a big part of celebrations?*
- *How are meals part of the life of our community of faith?*

Opening Prayer

Read the following prayer aloud, or use one of your own:

God of the Table,
>*You invite us to sit with you as you take the role of host and servant.*
>*You share the bread and cup with a table full of people*
>>*Who are often overcome by their fears.*
>*You kneel to wash the feet of those who misunderstand you.*
You kneel to wash the feet of those who will deny you.
We know the power of a meal among loved ones
>*And we know the challenge of living in love.*
Be present in our midst, Good Lord. Amen.

Learning Together

Video Study and Discussion

Say to the group: *We will continue our time together with a video featuring A.-J. Levine. A.-J. will talk about the primary themes of our session today: Jesus' last meal with his disciples, his betrayal, and the institution of the Eucharist. Make connections to what we have read together in her book. Then, we will discuss both the video and book together.*

Play the fifth track on the DVD, *Entering the Passion of Jesus, Session 5: The Last Supper: Risking the Loss of Friends* (running time is approximately 8–10 minutes).

Say to the group: *Let's keep in mind what A.-J. has said as we take a look at the book and examine these themes in light of our Lenten study.*

Book and Bible Study and Discussion

Remember the Passover

Read aloud the story of the Passover from Exodus 12:21-28:

> *Then Moses called all the elders of Israel and said to them, "Go, select lambs for your families, and slaughter the passover lamb. Take a bunch of hyssop, dip it in the blood that is in the basin, and touch the lintel and the two doorposts with the blood in the basin. None of you shall go outside the door of your house until morning. For the LORD will pass through to strike down the Egyptians; when he sees the blood on the lintel and on the two doorposts, the LORD will pass over that door and will not allow the destroyer to enter your houses to strike you down. You shall observe this rite as a perpetual ordinance for you and your children. When you come to the land that the LORD will give you, as he has promised, you shall keep this observance. And when your children ask you, 'What do you mean by this observance?' you shall say, 'It is the passover sacrifice to the LORD, for he passed over the houses of the Israelites in Egypt, when he struck down the Egyptians but spared our houses.'" And the people bowed down and worshiped.*

50

> *The Israelites went and did just as the* Lord *had commanded
> Moses and Aaron.*

Now divide into two small groups. Ask the first group to explore the
context for this passage. Using the first eleven chapters of Exodus and
chapter 5 of the study book as a resource, answer the following questions.
Give the group the index card you have prepared prior to the session with
these questions on it:

- *What was the oppression that concerned God?*
- *What was God doing to address it?*
- *What was the purpose of the Passover sacrifice?*

Ask the second group to explore how the Gospel of John talks about
Jesus. Using John 1:19-37 and chapter 5 of the study book as a resource,
answer the following questions. Give the group the index card you
prepared prior to the session with these questions on it:

- *What does John the Baptizer call Jesus in this passage?*
- *How does this title relate to the Passover story in Exodus 12?*
- *How does this understanding of who Jesus is change the
  understanding of the Passover offering?*

Read aloud Mark 14:66-72. Ask group members to imagine the scene
as you read it:

> *While Peter was below in the courtyard, one of the servant-
> girls of the high priest came by. When she saw Peter warming
> himself, she stared at him and said, "You also were with
> Jesus, the man from Nazareth." But he denied it, saying,
> "I do not know or understand what you are talking about."
> And he went out into the forecourt. Then the cock crowed.
> And the servant-girl, on seeing him, began again to say to the
> bystanders, "This man is one of them." But again he denied
> it. Then after a little while the bystanders again said to Peter,
> "Certainly you are one of them; for you are a Galilean." But he
> began to curse, and he swore an oath, "I do not know this man*

51

you are talking about." At that moment the cock crowed for the second time. Then Peter remembered that Jesus had said to him, "Before the cock crows twice, you will deny me three times." And he broke down and wept.

Distribute pieces of paper and drawing utensils to group members. Invite them to draw the scene as they imagine it. After allowing some minutes for this exercise, ask for volunteers to share their work. After the sharing time, thank the volunteers, then ask the group:

- *How do these drawings help us sense Peter's fear?*

On another piece of paper or the back of the drawing, have participants answer the following questions:

- *Did anyone ever say anything at a dinner that I found surprising, or even offensive? How did I react?*
- *How is my fear preventing me from speaking out on behalf of someone or something that is precious to me?*
- *If I were not afraid, what would I be doing?*

Assess the Role of Judas

Review the section of chapter 5 that talks about Judas. Ask:

- *How do the different Gospels talk about Judas?*
- *How do you understand the reasons why Judas betrayed Jesus?*

Consider Acts of Service

Ask the group to recall a time when someone did an unexpected act of service for them. Invite group members to turn to a neighbor and share their experience of that act.

After allowing a brief time for this exercise, draw the group back together and ask them to consider Jesus' act of washing his disciples' feet. Say to the group: *A.-J. notes that, in John's Gospel, Jesus' act of foot washing follows the act of the woman who anoints Jesus. How is Jesus' washing of the disciples' feet similar to the woman's act?*

Now ask the participants to picture one of their neighbors—someone living adjacent to them in a nearby house or apartment. Ask them to consider the following questions silently as you read them aloud:

- *What is my neighbor's name?*
- *What else do I know about this neighbor?*
- *What needs does my neighbor have that I might be able to meet?*
- *If my neighbor were to offer me a gift of service, how would it make me feel?*

Invite group members to identify and write down one thing they can do this week to deepen their relationship with their neighbors. Encourage participants to act on this commitment this week and to report back to the group how it went.

Wrapping Up

Closing Activity

Share Bread Around the Table

As a closing act, take the loaf of bread (and the gluten-free option, if you are using it) and invite persons to tear off a bit of bread as you pass it around the circle. (You can pass hand sanitizer around the circle ahead of the bread.)

Say to the group: *I have a good loaf of bread here (and a good gluten-free option, too). I'm going to pass it around the circle and invite you to tear off a piece of the bread to eat. This is* not *a communion meal, but various Christian groups have celebrated a love feast from time to time in which they share food and give testimony to how God is working in their lives. As you pull off some bread, I would invite you to share some way that you see God moving in your life through this Lenten journey with Jesus. If you want, you may pass by simply saying "pass."*

Begin the sharing yourself, modeling what you are asking individuals to do. Tear off a piece of bread and share a way that you sense God moving in your life. Then pass the loaf to the person on your left.

Closing Prayer

When the loaf has gone all the way around the circle, offer t
following prayer or one of your own:

Christ, you meet us in the midst of our many journeys
  And you call us to risk opening our lives to you and to our neighbors.
We break bread with one another and share our desire to be one body.
  We receive what you have to give, and go forth to give ourselves. Ame

Session 6

GETHSEMANE: RISKING TEMPTATION

Planning the Session

Session Goals

As a result of conversations and activities connected with this session, group members should begin to

- reflect on our journey through the Passion and how Jesus' entry into our lives entails risk and courage;
- assess nonviolence as a response to injustice;
- appreciate the importance of prayer, particularly as it helps us face the demands of our vocation; and
- understand the role of outsiders in revealing God's intentions in the Passion story.

Scriptural Foundation

[Jesus] came out and went, as was his custom, to the Mount of Olives; and the disciples followed him. When he reached the place, he said to them, "Pray that you may not come into the time of trial." Then he withdrew from them about a stone's

throw, knelt down, and prayed, "Father, if you are willing, remove this cup from me; yet, not my will but yours be done." Then an angel from heaven appeared to him and gave him strength. In his anguish he prayed more earnestly, and his sweat became like great drops of blood falling down on the ground. When he got up from prayer, he came to the disciples and found them sleeping because of grief, and he said to them, "Why are you sleeping? Get up and pray that you may not come into the time of trial."

Luke 22:39-46

Special Preparation

- Prepare the room with seating arranged in a circle so that everyone will be able to see one another.
- Create a small worship space in the center of the circle with visual reminders of God's presence. For this session that could include a cross and a picture of Jesus (or others) in prayer.
- Have available paper, pens, pencils, and other drawing materials.
- Also have available Bibles for those who may not have brought one.
- Prepare a sign that says *"Christians should always seek to find an alternative to violence."* and hang it on the wall in your meeting space.
- On two index cards, write the following (same words on each card):
  - *Read the following passages: Luke 22:47-53 and John 18:1-11.*
  - *Can you think of any time when you think a violent response (for example, protecting another person, being sent on a military mission) is warranted?*
  - *How does Jesus respond to the disciples when they react violently to his arrest?*
  - *What other stories from the Gospels do you recall that help us understand how Jesus views violence?*
  - *How will you defend the position you've been assigned?*

Getting Started

Opening Activity

Report Back on the Neighbor Commitment

If you used the exercise titled "Consider Acts of Service" last week, invite volunteers to share how they deepened their relationship with a neighbor in the past week. Ask: *What more does this encourage you to do to get to know your neighbor?*

Consider a Time When You Had to Take a Risk and Be Courageous

Invite group members to reflect on a time when they had to take a risk and be courageous. Ask them to remember the occasion silently as they consider the following questions:

- *What was the occasion?*
- *What fears did you have to overcome in order to act?*
- *Who helped you face your fears?*
- *If you prayed at that time, what did you say to God?*

Now invite a volunteer or two to share their stories. Say to the group: *In our final session we are going to consider Jesus praying in Gethsemane. Jesus prayed an honest prayer knowing the cost he would have to pay.*

Opening Prayer

Read the following prayer, or offer one of your own:

God of darkened gardens where our worst fears collect,
We have many things we would not do because they are hard.
We know the path to the empty tomb travels through the cross.
We know that those on the outside sometimes see more clearly
Than the insiders do.
We pray to stay near you, Lord,
And claim the courage of the Christ. Amen.

Learning Together

Video Study and Discussion

Say to the group: *We will continue our time together with a video featuring A.-J. Levine. A.-J. will talk about the primary themes of our session today: Jesus' prayerful agony in Gethsemane and his choice to accept God's will for him. Notice how A.-J. captures Jesus' emotional turmoil in her presentation. Make connections to what we have read together in her book. Then, we will discuss both the video and book together.*

Play the sixth track on the DVD, *Entering the Passion of Jesus*, Session 6: Gethsemane: Risking Temptation (running time is approximately 8–10 minutes).

Say to the group: *Let's keep in mind what A.-J. has said as we take a look at the book and examine these themes in light of our Lenten study.*

Book and Bible Study and Discussion

Reenact the Gethsemane Scene

Divide into two small groups to study the Gethsemane scene. Ask each group to read Mark 14:32-42. Have one group look at the passage from the perspective of Jesus and the other look at it from the perspectives of Peter, James, and John. Ask the "Jesus Group" to reflect using the following questions:

- *Besides what Jesus says, what might he be feeling and thinking in this scene?*
- *What tone of voice do you think he uses?*

Ask the "Disciples Group" to reflect using these questions:

- *The disciples don't speak in this passage, but what might they be feeling and thinking?*
- *Why do they fall asleep?*

Now ask each group to choose some volunteers to help reenact the scene. The Jesus Group will need one person to play Jesus and at least

e other person to give voice to what Jesus is thinking and feeling based
your conversation. The Disciples Group should choose three people to
ay the disciples and at least one other person to give voice to what Peter,
mes, and John are thinking. (If your groups are very small, the disciples
n be represented by one person.)

Now choose a narrator (or be the narrator yourself). Read through
e passage with the volunteer actors improvising the scene. Pause at
e places indicated and allow the volunteers who are giving voice to the
ternal monologue to speak:

> *They went to a place called Gethsemane; and he said to his
> disciples, "Sit here while I pray."*
> (Mark 14:32)

> *He took with him Peter and James and John, and began to
> be distressed and agitated. And he said to them, "I am deeply
> grieved, even to death; remain here, and keep awake."*
> (Mark 14:33-34)

AUSE FOR INTERNAL MONOLOGUES]

> *And going a little farther, he threw himself on the ground and
> prayed that, if it were possible, the hour might pass from him.
> He said, "Abba, Father, for you all things are possible; remove
> this cup from me; yet, not what I want, but what you want."*
> (Mark 14:35-36)

AUSE FOR JESUS' INTERNAL MONOLOGUE]

> *He came and found them sleeping; and he said to Peter,
> "Simon, are you asleep? Could you not keep awake one hour?
> Keep awake and pray that you may not come into the time of
> trial; the spirit indeed is willing, but the flesh is weak."*
> (Mark 14:37-38)

> *And again he went away and prayed, saying the same words.
> And once more he came and found them sleeping, for their
> eyes were very heavy; and they did not know what to say to
> him. He came a third time and said to them, "Are you still*

sleeping and taking your rest? Enough! The hour has come; the Son of Man is betrayed into the hands of sinners. Get up, let us be going. See, my betrayer is at hand."

(Mark 14:39-42)

[PAUSE FOR INTERNAL MONOLOGUES]

Thank the volunteers for their performance. Then ask the who group:

- *How does Jesus speak to God?*
- *How is this a model for our own prayers?*
- *What did Jesus risk when he brought his disciples to Gethsemane*
- *The disciples failed to stay awake. When have you felt that you have failed, and how have you felt God's redemption?*

Debate Nonviolence

Say to the group: A.-J. *says that when the disciples finally wake up, th respond with violence to those coming to arrest Jesus. Christians have alwa struggled with how to respond to injustices, including the use of violence.*

Direct the group's attention to the sign on the wall that you prepare earlier that reads: *Christians should always seek to find an alternative violence.* Tell the group that you are going to have a debate about th proposition, but they will not get to choose their position on the issue.

Divide the group into two, and assign one group the position defending the proposition on the wall. The other group will be arguin against it. Have the groups prepare by using the following direction and questions that you wrote down on two index cards prior the session:

- *Read the following passages: Luke 22:47-53 and John 18:1-11.*
- *Can you think of any time when you think a violent response (for example, protecting another person, being sent on a military mission) is warranted?*
- *How does Jesus respond to the disciples when they react violently to his arrest?*

- *What other stories from the Gospels do you recall that help us understand how Jesus views violence?*
- *How will you defend the position you've been assigned?*

After allowing the groups some time to work, bring the whole group back together and invite each to present its argument for 3 minutes. Remind them that the purpose of the debate is to get greater understanding, not to defeat the other side. Encourage respectful behavior. Following this, allow each group to ask questions of the other group. Give the group about 8 minutes for this question time.

Then call an end to the debate and ask:

- *What did you learn from having to present your side of the debate?*
- *How does Jesus respond to the violence done against him?*
- *What can we learn from his response?*

Write a Prayer

Say to the group: A.-J. *says that in some vocations, such as firefighting, policing, serving in the military, and treating infectious diseases, persons often have to take risks.* Ask the group:

- *What are the challenges and the risks faced by persons in these careers?*
- *What prayers do you imagine people of faith in these careers offer to God?*

Distribute paper and writing instruments and invite group members to write a prayer on behalf of people who face difficult situations and even death on a daily basis. Invite volunteers to share their prayers with the group. Consider sending some or all of the prayers to persons in these careers.

Wrapping Up

Closing Activity

Claim the Gifts of the Group

Since this is the last session, take some time to reflect on the gifts that you have received through this Lenten journey. Ask the group:

- *What is something new you learned from studying Jesus' Passion through this course?*
- *How do you feel challenged to take new risks on behalf of God's kingdom?*

Invite group members into a time of sharing. Join hands and have each person share one gift they have received from the group and one hope they have for the world or their lives. Model the sharing by going first. Tell the group that when you conclude, you will squeeze the hand of the person to your right, which will be the signal for the person to share. If people would like to pass, they can squeeze the hand of the person next to them without sharing.

Closing Prayer

After allowing time for the previous exercise, close with this prayer or one of your own:

We have come a long way with you, Jesus,
   And we have gifts to celebrate with these companions.
   We have watched you travel through expectations, disappointments, and betrayal.
   We have heard your heartfelt prayers.
We want to have the courage take the right risks, for we know the road of discipleship can be difficult.
So that we can walk courageously with you into the light of Easter
   As your people. Amen.

CPSIA information can be obtained
at www.ICGtesting.com
Printed in the USA
LVHW010058260219
608725LV00004B/4